WHO COACHES THE COACH?

3 Invaluable Lessons for Success in Coaching

Marilu Gonzalez,

M.A. Educ. Leadership

&

Ovidilio D. Vásquez,

High Content Speaker & Author of

The Parenting Book

Copyright © 2015
Speak Performance International, LLC
All rights reserved.
ISBN: 1508547653
ISBN-13: 978-1508547655

DEDICATION

When I first started my career I felt ready, I felt prepared. I had received an award for Physical education major of the year and was flown to New Orleans from Chicago, all expenses paid, to receive my award from the National Physical Education Professional Association. I had worked extremely hard to receive that honor. It was not my motivation, it was a reward, that is it. After that experience, I understood that rewards make sense because they offer an opportunity for excellence to collect. I met 40 other excellent physical education teachers across the country. It was an amazing experience, except it ended after that trip. If I would have known what I know now, my network would be entirely different.

This book is for all excellence seekers. All of my students and friends who have a strong longing to shine through the rough and rugged darkness they are surrounded by. This book is for the underdog, the business trailblazers, the people with fearless passions, and action movers. For my family, who have always pushed me towards excellence. For my father and mother, who longed to help us break through the walls of poverty. One thing was clear, that we needed to create the path ourselves. Here is my path.

TABLE OF CONTENTS

	Acknowledgments	IX
	Introduction	XI
1	First Lesson	13
2	Second Lesson	29
3	Third Lesson	39
4	Personal Development	53
5	Communication	67
6	Friendly Advice	77
7	Self-esteem	83
8	Building Character	87
9	Apprentice's Feelings	95
10	Motivation	103

No part of this book can be reproduced, stored in a retrieval system, nor transmitted by any means, either electronic, mechanical, photocopies, recording, or otherwise, without the express, written permission of the Publisher. No patent liability is assumed with respect to the use of the herein information, as the contents are presented solely for informational and entertainment purposes. Although extreme care has been utilized in the preparation of this book, neither the Publisher nor the authors assume any responsibility for errors or omissions. In addition, no responsibility is assumed for any damages that could be caused by the use of the information contained herein. Use it at your own risk. The information contained herein in *no way* replaces the advice of a competent, licensed professional of law, medicine, or mental health.

ACKNOWLEDGMENTS

I would like to thank my students, mentors, and friends who, through their compassion, have shared their life with me. I would also like to thank all of the coaches who have gallantly shared the field with me in competition. The richness of the experience extrapolates past the 90 minutes of game time.

I am forever grateful to my brothers, who graciously included me in this venture of coaching and my athletic director at South Suburban College Steve Ruzich. There are no words to describe your faith in me. Finally, I would like to thank my first and my greatest coach, TJ Shirley. I hope that you are enjoying God's grace in heaven. You deserve to be there.

INTRODUCTION

Who coaches the coach?

Have you ever had that question in your mind? I have always had this question in my mind. From the beginning of my career until now.

Who coaches the coach? The coach is held responsible for many different activities -building programs, motivating people, competing, and getting other coaches in line. Who really coaches the coach? I will share with you what you can do as a person, as a mentor, as the teacher, and as the coach, to be ready to lead and serve everyone you serve.

My friend, Ovidilio, is an author who is a coach and an apprentice to some of the most sought after professionals in his career. I invited him to share some of his fundamentals to help you build your students with the right mental attitude. His words carry weight.

FIRST LESSON

Learn from your student.

Every day, a student comes in with many different issues that they are either dealing with at the moment, or have dealt with. They come with so much richness of story and experience. You should be open as the coach to take in those lessons.

Your students, regardless of their age. Regardless of how much experience they have within your sport. Regardless of their knowledge within the activity that they are doing. You have to be open as a coach.

Your first coaching session is definitely going to be restrained. Being able to adapt, being able to help, and being resourceful with your students will make you a better coach. It will make you a better competitor.

The experience will give you a format or a plan that can be the foundation of what your goals are. It will even give you a hint of how to reach those goals, and how to surpass them.

The first lesson, and maybe the most important lesson, is: Be open to learn from your students. Learn from every person you come across. Learn the good and the bad. Learn for the purpose of serving. That means that within yourself, within your conscience, you have to be awake. You have to communicate. You have to be supportive.

"The greatest among you will be your servant."
~Matthew 3:11

Make sure that every day you are in command, it is almost like you renew your state of mind. Your students will have the opportunity to share what they have learned with you. They will even tell you what their goals are and that can definitely inspire you to become a better coach.

I came to the realization because it did not matter what I thought about my students. It did not matter what my plan was throughout the seasons. Of the hundreds of students who I have coached at many different levels, if they were not part of that planning process, if they had no ownership over the goals, the program itself would be a waste of time.

If you are willing to be open, if you are willing to include them in the process and to not only include their ambitions and their aspirations, but also their experience, you nourish their prior knowledge. Use their knowledge and potential to build on that within your program.

You will accomplish much more. You will not be battling yourself psychologically. Include them in the process, let them know. When they are part of the leadership, they can take ownership of the program. Let it become theirs, so you are no longer a dictator. You are no longer responsible for everything, the routine, the art bags, the equipment.

You know the plans. If you have your students giving you the answers, the questions can be the answers. The answers can be the questions. It is up to your students you know to be able to also be open to participate.

You have to be on the same level of the students and the students need to raise themselves and build themselves up to be at your level.

Be open to learn from your students. Be resourceful because that will make you a better coach. Be awake, be able to communicate, and be supportive. Having coached thousands of students, I have discovered how to implement this for a student or an apprentice, an apprentice who has come from a different country with a different background than yours.

Soccer is a world sport. Soccer is played in underprivileged societies as privileged societies most people play the sport. Soccer does that for everyone. I have met so many and even been able to coach students who don't speak English. It all goes back to you having to be open, resourceful, and willing to include everyone, where you take the attitude of inclusiveness instead of being evict. Even if you do that and you are able to create an environment that supports your student.

Your gain will gain a lot more in very different realms, whether it is personal, spiritual, and competitive. Feeding the idea that this is a cohesive group effort is much better than having such a rigid thing set in stone, where it's either my way or the highway.

In my experience with many successful coaches, they have always been extremely flexible in their perspective field. Not only in terms of discipline but also within the sport because we go to different countries and study different ways of organizing teams and playing to be victorious.

Every country has their own way, their own style, and their own perspective. When you get the opportunity to have different people from different countries on your team, you are at an advantage. The experience and resource of diversity is game changing. It is positive, you know that resourcefulness is great.

Being open to learning from your student does not only apply to sports. It also applies when you are coaching apprentices in business, school, finance, marketing, and accounting. These lessons also apply to these types of coaching. I have always told my students to keep an open mind, strong heart, a positive attitude, and work ethic when playing soccer. Those qualities are very much needed in the market place and they will be prepared for it.

You must know that my plan after graduating out of college was not to become a central coach, it was to become an indicator. I was actually doing real estate at time. When I was offered the opportunity to coach, I took it more as a crash route, donating my time more than actually trying to build programs. Has this ever happened to you or other coach you know?

As I was trying to teach myself to build these programs starting from the bottom, there was very little organization. I used many different business tactics and ways to organize my team. I was able to learn those from books, business people, and other online resources.

Keep in mind, the lessons learned through sports can be adapted to businesses and other settings. I strongly believe in it. I tell my students, *"Sports is just a practice, a practice opportunity for how you will deal with real life."* Eerything you teach your students on your field can transfer over: how you deal with adversity, how you deal with conflict, how disciplined you are.

It is good practice, being on the field is good practice. When you encounter a student who is being bullied, how do you deal with that? Do you ignore it? Do you just try to let time pass? Do you fight back? Do you just make eye contact or do you exchange words?

It is something you can prepare in your students. Develop their mindset. Tell them something like, "It can happen to you somewhere else. Here, you can practice and it is safe to practice." Practice being a world-class team player, a disciplined person, a go-getter. These lessons and skills will serve your students in many different realms of life.

I have coached hundreds of students, as well as apprentices who I have had the opportunity meet. Here is one of the success stories about an apprentice I coached, who went on and became successful in her chosen field.

I chose this student because I learned from her that the offers or the opportunities you have are not always going to be for you. This young lady was a straight "A" student in high school. She was very shy. She didn't have confidence and communication skills.

Brenda was very focused, disciplined, honest, and loyal, with integrity. When she went away to school, she received an opportunity to play soccer at a Division III school. She quickly realized that the opportunities she had academically were not the same in that school. It was definitely there through sports, but she was never expecting to get that opportunity through sports.

Brenda started playing soccer later on in her life, but because of her work ethic, she was able to catch on quickly. She received that opportunity, but she realized early enough that it was not for her. She made a decision to go back to community college, and to playing with my team for two more years.

Brenda maintained a 4.0 and was a scholarship recepient to the University to New York City. Within a year and a half, she graduated and became a certified public accountant. Her life changed dramatically. She comes from a low economic household and now she is generating more income than her mother, her father, and her brother together. She comes back all the time.

Brenda taught me to work really hard, but that not all opportunities are for us. We need to look for the best opportunities out there. In terms of the big picture, her whole life, she needed to be where she wanted to be. Her courage was noteworthy. She continues to have courage. She is working in downtown Chicago now in a big company.

Brenda is developing her communication skills. She practices personal development all the time. I have learned so much from her in terms of not to be pushing my students to do specific things. They have to choose what they want to do. No matter what, their lives are going to unfold in a positive way because of all of the fundamental skills for success like work ethic, honesty, and just having a wide vision and being fearless.

It did not really matter what I thought. Because I always wanted to push my kids to go to the Division I school or to take that soccer scholarship, that opportunity, and she taught me that they already have the fundamental skills and they need to seek their own opportunities. What are some of the lessons you have learned from your apprentices?

Brenda knew that just because you are preparing them for one field does not mean life has prepared them for that field, too. They can just apply the same fundamentals you have taught them through coaching. They can take them to a different field where they feel most comfortable.

"You can have everything in life you want, if you will just help enough other people get what they want."
~Zig Ziglar

Write down strategies that have allowed you to *learn from your student* and some ideas on how you could learn even more from them and vice versa.

FIRST LESSON

Write down strategies that have allowed you to *learn from your student and some ideas* on how you could learn even more from them and vice versa.

Write down strategies that have allowed you to *learn from your student* and some ideas on how you could learn even more from them and vice versa.

FIRST LESSON — Who Coaches The Coach?

Write down strategies that have allowed you to *learn from your student* and some ideas on how you could learn even more from them and vice versa.

Write down for strategies that have allowed you to *learn from your student* and some ideas on how you could learn even more from them and vice versa.

SECOND LESSON

Learn from your losses.

I see this often in personal development involved. Sometimes you have to lose to win, right? As coaches, we tend attach a great deal of emotions to either winning or losing. You need to learn from both. They are both as valuable. You need to be able to turn around look back and ask, "Okay, what worked? What works?"

If this is working with the group that you are working with, you should make sure you are maintaining, supporting, and promoting that. You cannot forget about what worked. You must remember how you won, especially when you're talking about championships. Do not become overwhelmed with emotion.

Remember the thought processes or the procedures you used to get to where you are now. When you lose, you tend to be over analytic. Like, "What just happened?" That is exactly what you say to yourself when you are done coaching.

Do not become overwhelmed, especially when you were expected to win. When you expected a victory, it's like, "Okay, what just happened here? Let me look back." Then, you go minute by minute. Sometimes you go second by second of what just happened. I believe you should maintain the same positive, winning attitude all the time.

Take time to reflect and go back minute by minute, second by second of what worked, always seeking the positive in both the winning and losing. You cannot forget how you won because you need to be able to repeat that, not just for the team you are working with, but you also have to be able to experience the same with all the other groups.

You can be analytical about losing. But, also be analytical about winning. When I was fresh out of college, I graduated with a physical education degree. I was recruited right away to coach. I actually really believed in the theories and everything I learned in college. I was given the opportunity to coach a group of little boys. I would say, "They were born talented. They were born to play soccer."

When I started, I had never played soccer before. I had coached some other teams. I already knew when I first saw them. The first day I saw these kids together, *I already knew their destination was greatness*. I could already see it. What do you see in your student?

In those first couple of days I spent time with them, it was a matter of making sure I could make game changing decisions. What is your strategy? Are your decisions game changing? I learned very quickly. I knew could not be the only one doing it this way. The kids had to also be be equipped with that process of being able to make game changing decisions themselves.

Figure out how to get the kids to focus. Because children have a very hard time focusing their attention, make everything positive and everything fun. Break skills down into smaller parts and work hard on that. Master those fundamental skills and then apply them to the game. Let the kids do the work themselves. The organization of the team and even the organization of the parents will sometimes be your job.

I made sure I tried really hard to perfect that. I was able to equip them with the capability of doing more. There were many times I coached my kids for close to eight years. I still coach them now. You will have some students like that. It's been 10 years since we started. Some of my kids are coming back to work with some of my Division I training.

They are getting started. I still see that their thought processes are definitely toward being game changers and making the right decisions. Most of them were 5 to 6 years old when they started. Now they are 15 to 16 years old and some of them are going across the country. I have one who is actually at a residential soccer school. She goes to a high school where they eat, breathe, and sleep soccer. They teach them their courses during the day, but most of the time you know she is spending on the soccer field.

What is really more important is the relationship they have with each other. Their relationship is amazing, which is very difficult to find in teenagers. Remember, most teenagers are very exclusive in their social environment and the friends they have.

They have one or two friends and when I see them now, it is amazing. They are able to get along so well. There are eighteen of them. Their lives are much richer because they have a strong bond they created as children. They have it now in their teenage years, where, as a group, they are able to accomplish much more.

It is the attitude of inclusiveness. They include everyone they knew from the beginning and that is also applied to the fundamentals you have taught. This is part of the lesson you can apply in your students' lives. Learn from your students. We are always teaching someone, either consciously or unconsciously.

People are always learning from us and we have to go through winning situations and losing situations. We have to learn how to analyze those moments and to be able to turn things around if they're not looking the way we were expecting it to.

SECOND LESSON

Write down strategies that have allowed you to *learn from your losses* and some ideas on how you could learn even more.

Write down strategies that have allowed you to *learn from your losses* and some ideas on how you could learn even more.

SECOND LESSON

Write down strategies that have allowed you to *learn from your losses* and some ideas on how you could learn even more.

Write down strategies that have allowed you to *learn from your losses* and some ideas on how you could learn even more.

SECOND LESSON
Who Coaches The Coach?

Write down strategies that have allowed you to *learn from your losses* and some ideas on how you could learn even more.

THIRD LESSON

Go out and look outside of your environment.

It took me a lot of experience to be able to wholeheartedly accept it as something that needed to be a norm in my life. As coach, being at the level of leadership where there are many responsibilities and expectations should be a part of the norm. It took me a while to realize that I needed to go out and look outside of my environment. I needed to stop being so nearsighted and then choose mentorship out of my comfort zone.

On a daily basis, get out and search for it. *"Ask, and it shall be given you; seek, and ye shall find; knock, and it shall be opened unto you." Matthew 7:7* Social media is brilliant for this. You are able to connect with people all around the world. Genuinely try and establish a mentor-mentee relationship with people across the world.

Great people are willing to share because there is just not enough personal experience around you to be able to sustain yourself within the competition. Being stress-free is not even a possibility when you are deep into competition.

You must have that network of people even outside of your sports. Business leaders have been such great mentors for me in coaching soccer. Motivational speakers have become a fundamental part of my life, where it is a daily dose, a tremendous daily dose. A lot of the motivational material I use, I use it with my students, too. I encourage you to do the same.

They appreciate it a lot because they are able to try and understand what they are going through, psychologically speaking. The motivational material is a blessing to them. They are able to understand and it actually makes a direct impact on how they perform. They are looking at the world with an open mind and with their eyes. Not only what is in front of you but what is far away can also make a profound impact on your wins and losses.

It took me a while to realize that and it might also take you a while. Find mentors who are always going to be supportive and positive.

"You are the average of the five people you spend the most time with." ~Jim Rohn

You may have the people who are very critical or judgmental, and they are very important, too, because sometimes we tend to have a perspective, a perception of ourselves that is a fantasy. Sometimes it is not how we truly are in reality. It is important to be able to go out there and have other people get that first impression. Be open to receive feedback, it helps you grow even more.

Growing into a broader environment where you can learn and expand more, then, bringin it back home, it creates a ripple effect. Share it with your students and then they will be able to use it themselves. Leading by example, going outside of your comfort zone, and bringing value, your student will use it within their team and that could be also applied either in a sports setting, in a professional setting, or even in a classroom setting.

With the technology we have at our hands, there is so much opportunity and creativity that you can apply to be able to make those connections. Establish a strong relationship with someone who lives thousands of miles away from you.

That person can be so far away from you but can be very crucial in the success of your business team, your soccer team, or in your classroom.

I am sure that in the past, you went out of your comfort zone, doing something you probably never did. You said, *"I'm going for it."* Then, you made that personal contact with someone who provided you some values you could bring back home. If so, contact that person if possible and thank them. Send them a text, email, a letter, or give them a call and thank them sincerely.

When value is shared with me, I bring it home. I teach my kids the same fundamentals. You tend to be more courageous and start thinking out-of-the-box when you have that personal feeling of wanting success. I was able to go out and meet the coaches from around the country. Then, after that, I went international and I have this good friend who lives in Manchester, England. Every time I need to come up with a certain way to manage my groups, or to motivate them, not only them but to organize my coaching lessons, I am able to talk to him.

He is someone I met when I took my son to Northwestern University coaching camp. I met this coach, who was amazing, and he was able to engage twenty 7-year-old participants in the camp for four hours, nonstop. The most he did was give them water breaks.

When he first walked in, I looked at him and I was just like, "There is no way this guy is going to be able to keep these seven-year-old little boys engaged for four hours. How is he going to do that?"

I was a physical education teacher at a high school and it is difficult to keep high school students motivated for 45 minutes. I was like, "How is this guy going to do this?" By looking at my son, I could see my son was full of energy. It is very difficult for him to follow directions the first time.

Well, he did it. He did it! He was nonstop for four hours, an incredible teacher. He had all types of little small routines concepts he applied. His energy was contagious. The kids were as motivated as him throughout the entire four hours and it was absolutely amazing to me. I said, *"Coach, I really like your style, you have to teach me how to be like this."*

I had never seen anyone do that before. He is also a physical education teacher in England. He teaches middle school students in England. He is been such a great resource, where, many times, I would ask for his guidance when I have a very difficult group. Then, he just tells me what he does and it has been phenomenal. Now my son is already 12 years old.

I was only able to see him coach one summer, for that one season, but he has been in my coaching life since my son was seven. He has made such a great difference in the things I do and the way I formulate the practices, even the way I coach my game.

I believe he unconsciously was learning from his students at that one point where he kept them engaged. He was learning whether they were engaged or not, then, probably changed his tactics and I bet he was learning whether he was going to win or lose in these four hours to get them and keep them engaged. He was probably looking out of his comfort zone because there he was, an adult trying to deal with twenty 7 year old kids. I believe he was applying these three life lessons for success in coaching.

I would like you to keep to your heart and ponder in your mind. You know when you are out there, especially as a new leader. As a new or seasoned coach, you are out there and you are trying to establish your philosophy of coaching. You can write it down as much as you want; life is actually trying to test your philosophy. Remember these three life lessons.

The wins and the losses, they do not really let you know or gauge if you are going in the right direction or not. They also do not tell you if you are a good coach or not. People will tell you if you are a good coach or not. Your students will tell you if you are a good coach or not.

Listen to your students very closely. Listen to your mentors. Accept and embrace the necessary changes they are telling you about. If they are telling you that you are phenomenal at fitness training, then you are phenomenal at fitness training. If they are telling you that you work great with smaller children, then you work great with younger children.

Just listen, that coaches you, that is your education. That is who coaches the coach and the people you are serving, the people who are genuinely interested in seeing you succeed.

I have shared with you value that can be applied immediately. This content is dear to me. These experiences have transformed me into a person of better character. My wish for you is that you find and share the value in this book. Be willing to take the lip. Failure is part of the process. Failure is in a event, not a person.

My very good friend, Ovidilio, will share with you more strategies, tools, and ideas on how to become even better coach. He shares his value from a student's perspective. He is mentored by some of the most successful people in his field. You will find this young man to have a promising future because of what he does today.

THIRD LESSON — Who Coaches The Coach?

Write down strategies that have allowed you to *go out and look outside your environment* and some ideas on how you could do it even more.

Write down strategies that have allowed you to *go out and look outside your environment* and some ideas on how you could do it even more.

THIRD LESSON

Write down strategies that have allowed you to *go out and look outside your environment* and some ideas on how you could do it even more.

Write down strategies that have allowed you to *go out and look outside your environment* and some ideas on how you could do it even more.

THIRD LESSON

Write down strategies that have allowed you to *go out and look outside your environment* and some ideas on how you could do it even more.

Thank you for making the investment in adding more value to yourself. I admire coaches and mentors who go out and seek new ways to do better. You are a champion. The fact that you are now reading this book puts you at a higher level than 80% percent of the rest of America.

Do you remember a time when you had a coach or mentor, when you said, "Wow, I am blessed to have this person teaching me."? Maybe not the exact words but somewhat similar. If you answered "Yes", you know how gratifying it feels to have a coach who is very valuable and knowledgeable.

I am a mentee to some of the most successful people in my profession. And as a student to them, I am going to share with you some ideas and strategies I believe will enhance your endeavors. The content I will share with you did not come only from me. The content is a collection of what I have learned from others, in my own words. I applaud you for taking the time to read this book and I appreciate you.

~Ovidilio D. Vásquez

PERSONAL DEVELOPMENT

How do I become more successful in coaching?

The key answer to this question is: You must educate yourself first to educate others. By reading this book, you are enhancing your skills on coaching success. You will improve the quality of your relationship with your apprentice by applying what I will share with you in this quick, but powerful section of book. Enjoy!

First, let me identify "success" in the words of the great Earl Nightingale, ***"Success is the progressive realization of a worthy ideal."*** Nightingale was the world's renowned self-development guru and author of *The Strangest Secret in the World*, *Lead the Field*, and countless invaluable productions that have changed millions of lives, including mine.

Once you know what it is you are looking for, you can find it easier. When you want to travel to X city, most people use Google Maps, but unless you identify where you are traveling from, it will not tell you how to get to point B.

To be more successful, I also have been applying advice from Mr. Warren Buffett

Warren Buffett

On Earnings

Never depend on a single income. Make an investment to create a second source.

On Spending
If you buy things you do not need, soon, you will have to sell things you need.

On Savings
Do not save what is left after spending, but spend what is left after saving.

On Taking Risks
Never test the depth of a river with both feet.

On Investment
Do not put all eggs in one basket

On Expectation
Honesty is a very expensive gift. Do not expect it from cheap people.

> ***"Whether you think you can, or you think you can't – you're right."-Henry Ford***

When it comes to success, Zig Ziglar's advice is to think of the most successful person you know. It could be a man, a woman, your parents, son, daughter, or neighbor, a preacher, a sales person, a teacher, a politician, or a writer… you get the idea.

This person has to be someone who, if you cannot be you, you would say, *"I want to be her"* or *"I want to be him."* Do not include a rich coach just because he or she is rich. Many people are rich in money and wealth but very poor in love. Think about what the qualities are that make that coach successful.

Some qualities could be: a coach with a positive mental attitude, with great faith, a desire to achieve more, and with enthusiasm. A coach who is a good listener with a good sense of humor, a coach who has integrity, who is consistent, who has love in their life, who is sincere, who is an encourager, a coach who is a hard worker, and the list can continue.

Now, think about this: are you a coach who practices these qualities on a daily basis? Are you working on acquiring or improving these qualities? When you apply some effort in your daily routine to become someone with these qualities, a compound effect begins to take effect.

Think about this: if a person eats a burger with a big soda on a daily basis, does that person become BIG in the first two weeks for eating the same portion every day? Probably not, but because he or she does it daily, the compound effect eventually kicks in and the person starts getting BIG.

Once they are in that stage, more problems begin to occur. As my good friend, Justin Mendez, keynote speaker, would say in his "Mental Breakfast" speech, *"As days add up to weeks, weeks add up to months, and months add up to years… We reap the bountiful harvest of our habits."*

What habits are you implementing to get you toward being a more successful coach? The people you choose as a role model, what habits do they have? Are you ready to say goodbye to some of your habits and say hello to better ones?

> *"You have made some mistakes and you may not be where you want to be... but that has nothing to do with your future."*
>
> *~Zig Ziglar*

Napoleon Hill, in his book, *Think and Grow Rich*, mentioned the importance of a mission statement. Every successful person carries one with them, whic serves as a focus point. I have included my mission statement I developed when I made a firm decision to become what I desired.

Feel free to copy my mission statement and edit it so it fits your own situation.

"Goal: To Get Financially Rewarded To Speak by July 1st 2013

I'm willing to read every day all the material that's needed to deliver a speech according to the requested topic. I'm willing give up Family Guy and instead, grow and expand my mind in positive terms so I can be able to be, do, and have more of that which I desire.

I'm willing to discipline myself in various situations so I can make the choices I have to make instead of choices I want to make. I'm open to all possibilities and willing to go through all the procedures and obstacles that might come along.

I'm willing to consciously think and act positive toward all situations in life, for I know and trust that everything that's happening, and will happen, is for my own good.

I'm willing to share 10% of my time and income so I can make an impact in my greater community. I'm committed to stay consistent and work hard in a smart way to see all these goals through and finally achieve my desired outcome. I trust and know that I have what it takes; therefore, my goal is closer than I can currently imagine.

My purpose is to express my willingness to accept change, willingness to work hard, and willingness to go the extra mile by being committed to do things differently, by being consistent with labor, and by going beyond my goals to free up one extra day a week for family/personal time, become a motivational speaker, have more happiness and joy in life, and obtain at least $100,000.00 by 12/19/2013."

I did not reach my goal of getting the $100k but I did reach my goal of being a professional speaker in 2013. When you are working toward your personal goals, it is not going to be easy.

Easy is not always on the menu. It is hard and it is worth it. Be patient, be smart, be persistent, be a good apprentice, and above all, keep the faith. Remember, Winston Churchill said, **"Never, ever, ever, ever, ever, give up."**

Share this on Facebook and Twitter: #OVinspires @ OVinspires

"Hang around with people who will hold you accountable for your words! People who dream bigger than you! People who earn more than you! People who are smarter than you! Hang around those people and be bold enough to ask for help. But, make it a WIN-WIN situation. Be willing to humble yourself and serve!"
~Ovidilio D. Vasquez

I will also tell you this on the coaching side of success. Do not aim for perfection. No one is perfect; do not torture yourself with an impossibly high bar for coaching success. Be confident with your coaching skills. You are a gifted coach, embrace it.

Make an effort to ignore the pressure sometimes, and you may find yourself a more relaxed coach. Remember: slow and steady. Enjoy every moment of it. Life is made up of memorable moments. Prepare yourself every day.

"It is better to be prepared for an opportunity and not have one than to have an opportunity and not be prepared."
~Whitney M. Young, Jr.

Record your important thoughts and ideas on how to improve on your **Personal Development**

PERSONAL DEVELOPMENT

Record your important thoughts and ideas on how to improve on your **Personal Development**

Record your important thoughts and ideas on how to improve on your **Personal Development**

PERSONAL DEVELOPMENT

Record your important thoughts and ideas on how to improve on your **Personal Development**

Record your important thoughts and ideas on how to improve on your **Personal Development**

COMMUNICATION

How do I build a stronger communication with my apprentice?

Sit down and make a list of questions that you would genuinely want to know the answer to.

Here are some examples:

Who is your best friend?
What makes him/her your best friend?
Who is someone in your school you have a hard time getting along with?
Why do you think that happens?
Who is your favorite teacher?
Why is he/she your favorite teacher?
Who is your worst teacher?
Why is he/she your worst teacher?
What are you looking forward to?
As a team, where would you like to go on field trip?
What would we do?
What is your favorite song?

Now ask them to play their favorite song for you. Ask why that song means so much to them. The goal of this is for you to get in their mind and understand what is going on. Practice not talking, ask the question and listen actively. Your apprentice will begin to realize that you truly are interested in them, even more than their own parents sometimes and they will appreciate it.

Being a coach is being a student of your apprentice. Be with them. They need time with you. Even if they do not say it, your apprentice needs you to be there when no one else is. As you know, sometimes, they have problems at home and have no one to truly trust and open up to.

Personally, sometimesm I do not want to ask my mentor, even if I feel lost, even if I know I need help. Days go by and I do not reach out to my coach. Then, my mentors contact me and ask, "Is everything okay? How are you doing?" My response is: "I did not know if you were busy so I did not ask or reach out for guidance."

My point is that even I, a professional, still make the mistake of not asking when I have to or want to. So, what do you think is going through your apprentice's mind? If they do not call you, you call them.

Ask questions or even just to say, "Hey, champion, I wanted to see how you are doing and let you know that I care about you." That can make the whole difference between an apprentice who will perform with his heart for you and one who will not. Build the champion in your apprentice and let them know they are champions before they can even see it.

Record your important thoughts and ideas on how to improve your **Communication.**
Perhaps add a list of questions to ask.

COMMUNICATION

Record your important thoughts and ideas on how to improve your **Communication.**
Perhaps add a list of questions to ask.

Record your important thoughts and ideas on how to improve your **Communication.**
Perhaps add a list of questions to ask.

COMMUNICATION

Record your important thoughts and ideas on how to improve your **Communication**.
Perhaps add a list of questions to ask.

Record your important thoughts and ideas on how to improve your **Communication.**
Perhaps add a list of questions to ask.

FRIENDLY ADVICE

How do I give more friendly advice?

"The solution of all adult problems tomorrow depends in large measure upon the way our children grow up today."
~Margaret Mead, Anthropologist

Here is a friendly advice you can give your apprentice:

Life is like a Camera
FOCUS *on what is important.*
CAPTURE *the good times.*
DEVELOP *from the negatives.*
And if things do not work out… Just take another
SHOT.

I will refer again to Zig Ziglar's teachings. He states that for a coach to understand their kids, a coach needs to get down to their kid's intellectual level, and yet lead them.

Your apprentice needs a coach who has mature judgment and who will make all decisions based on the best interests of the apprentice. Not what the kid wants, but what he or she needs. They need preparedness, discipline, guidance, and a friend. You are not here to please your kids, you are here to guide, to direct, and to encourage them.

If your apprentice does not want to obey when you give him instruction, explain that you were entrusted by his parents and teachers to guide him and that is what you are going to do. But, remember to do it in a very friendly manner. You are his coach. Strategize on how to approach this situation before it even happens. As Brian Tracy would say, be one the main source of love for your kids. Once they know that, they are more likely to obey your rules.

Record your important thoughts and ideas on how to give **friendly advice** to your apprentice

FRIENDLY ADVICE

Record your important thoughts and ideas on how to give **friendly advice** to your apprentice

Record your important thoughts and ideas on how to give **friendly advice** to your apprentice

FRIENDLY ADVICE

Record your important thoughts and ideas on how to give **friendly advice** to your apprentice

SELF-ESTEEM

How do I elevate my kids' self-esteem?

Share this with your kids:

If an egg is broken by outside forces, life ends. If an egg is broken by an inside force, life begins. Great things always happen from inside.

Your kids need to learn and be aware of the importance of their thoughts and feelings about themselves. You will now be able to provide support for them to grow their self-esteem to higher levels.

This will lead to better performance, better grades, better attitude, and better relationships outside and at home. Make sure to encourage them to accept themselves, to value themselves, to forgive themselves, to bless themselves, to trust themselves, to love themselves, and to empower themselves.

Share this on Facebook and Twitter: #OVinspires @OVinspires

Self-esteem is not about bragging. It is about getting to know what you are good at and not so good at.

I want to share with you a self-talk I learned from some of my virtual mentors. The method of Autosuggestion is the hypnotic or subconscious adoption of an idea that one has originated oneself, e.g., through repetition of verbal statements to oneself to change behavior.

This self-talk will help you and your apprentice to increase self-esteem. Read it in the morning and afternoon every day. Read it in front of a mirror to make a greater impact. Remember, the eyes are the windows to the soul.

When reading these lines, touch your heart. Feelings

are the most important factor to every human being.

1. *I deeply and completely love myself.*
2. *I believe in myself apart from others' opinions.*
3. *I feel good about taking care of my own needs.*
4. *I am comfortable being myself around others.*
5. *I am a unique and valuable person just as I am.*
6. *I am becoming more and more confident.*
7. *I love myself just the way I am.*
8. *I like the way I handle challenges.*
9. *I feel good and good is attracted to me.*
10. *I openly express my needs and feelings.*
11. *I am my own unique self — special, creative, and wonderful.*
12. *I love and accept myself.*
13. *I am healthy and happy.*
14. *I am inherently worthy as a person.*
15. *I accept and learn from my mistakes.*

SELF-ESTEEM

Who Coaches The Coach?

Sometimes the chains that prevent us from being free are more mental than physical.

BUILDING CHARACTER

How do I build my kids' positive character?

"We may not be able to prepare the future for our children, but we can at least prepare our children for the future."
~Franklin D. Roosevelt

Here are 3 rules to teach your kids so they can be a person of good character.

First: *teach them not to forget the person who helps them.*
Second: *teach them not to hate the person who loves them.*
Third: *teach them not to cheat the person who trusts them.*

Life is simple. You can teach your kids those three rules and you are on your way to training and developing kids with great character.

You will build your kids' character by also teaching about compassion in the team. This will help you train a positive kid who may be surrounded negative world, even at home sometimes. Remember, your apprentice pays more attention to what you do than what you say.

Here is a story I read in

www.MoralStories.org

Making Relationships Special

"When I was a kid, my mom liked to make breakfast food for dinner every now and then. And I remember one night in particular when she had made dinner after a long, hard day at work. On that evening so long ago, my mom placed a plate of eggs, sausage, and extremely burned biscuits in front of my dad. I remember waiting to see if anyone noticed! Yet all Dad did was reached for his biscuit, smile at my mom and ask me how my day was at school. I don't remember what I told him that night, but I do remember watching him smear butter and jelly on that biscuit and eat every bite!

When I got up from the table that evening, I remember hearing my mom apologize to my dad for burning the biscuits. And I'll never forget what he said: "Honey, I love burned biscuits."

Later that night, I went to kiss Daddy good night and I asked him if he really liked his biscuits burned. He wrapped me in his arms and said, "Your momma put in a hard day at work today and she's real tired. And besides, a little burned biscuit never hurt anyone!"

Moral: Life is full of imperfect things and imperfect people. I'm not the best at everything; I forget birthdays, and anniversaries just like everyone else. But, what I have learned over the years is learning to accept each other's faults, and choosing to celebrate each other's differences, is one of the most important keys to creating a healthy, growing, and lasting relationship.

The person who submitted this story is *anonymous*.

Here is a valuable piece of content that you can share with your students. They can use it as self-talk. Sometimes, besides what you tell them, the only positive words they will hear are the ones they tell themselves.

"I CHOOSE"

I choose to live by choice, not by chance,
To be motivated, not manipulated,
To be useful, not used,
To make changes, not excuses,
To excel, not compete.
I choose great character, not bad character,
I choose to listen to my inner voice,
not to the random opinions of others.
I choose to do the things others won't so I can continue to do the things they can't.
Because, if I continue doing what I have been doing,
I will keep getting what I have been getting.
Therefore, I will act for best of my personal interest.

Author: Unknown

Record your important thoughts and ideas on how to help your kids in building character

Record your important thoughts and ideas on how to help your kids in building character

Record your important thoughts and ideas on how to help your kids in building character

BUILDING CHARACTER

Record your important thoughts and ideas on how to help your kids in building character

APPRENTICE'S FEELINGS

How Do I Make My Kids Feel Good?

"Tough times never last, tough people always do."
~**Robert Herjavec,** billionaire investor from ABC's TV Hit Show Shark Tank

A big part of positive coaching is helping your apprentice feel good about himself by nurturing his self-esteem without going overboard. It is important to realize that this does not come from catering to his every wish or showering him with insincere flattery, but by praising their legitimate accomplishments.

Keep in mind that these accomplishments can be simple, depending on your apprentice's age and skill level. It also comes from using care when admonishing your child, and refraining from using demeaning or demoralizing words in your instruction.

It is important to note that kids need to be allowed to do things on their own before you can praise them for the act, so do not be afraid to let your kids experience age-appropriate independence as often as possible. They will become better team players.

Another part of positive coaching includes catching your kids in the act of obedience, compassion, or courtesy. It is amazing how many times every day that their parents will say **"No"** or **"Don't"** instead of **"Yes"** and **"Do"**. Many parents will tiptoe past the obedience scene so they do not disrupt the harmony that is playing out inside. But, you are their coach, you have been prepared for this, you know what will make an impact in your apprentice's life, do it.

A better choice can be to stop and praise your kids for showing kindness toward his team member and let him know how much you appreciate the fact that he takes responsibilities so seriously, even if it is a small act, like bringing in the training equipment.

This part of positive coaching can also encompass the rewards for the obvious behaviors as well, such as a trip to see some professional team play locally.

I added this quote as extra bonus for this chapter. It was written by the great Mark Twain. It will help you and your kids avoid unwanted conversations that may end up hurting your or his feelings.

"Never argue with stupid people, they will drag you down to their level and then beat you with experience."

~Mark Twain

Be Positive: No surprise here, coaches who express negative emotions toward their kids or handle them roughly are likely to find themselves with aggressive kids. That is bad news, because behavioral aggression at different ages is linked to aggression later in life, even toward future romantic partners.

If you find yourself in a cycle of the angry coach, angry apprentice, angrier coach, try to break free. It will ease your problems in the long run.

I am not a coach, I am an apprentice. A lot of coaches think they know the best way to train an apprentice. It turns out that coaching is not one-size-fits-all. Kids whose coaches tailor their coaching style to the kids' personality have half the anxiety and depression of their peers with more rigid coaches.

Record your important thoughts and ideas on how to help your kids feel good, better, and best!

APPRENTICE'S FEELINGS — Who Coaches The Coach?

Record your important thoughts and ideas on how to help your kids feel good, better, and best!

Record your important thoughts and ideas on how to help your kids feel good, better, and best!

MOTIVATION

Motivation is like bathing. It does not last forever. That is the main reason why Zig Ziglar recommends it every day.

Every time I deliver a motivational workshop to parents on how to raise positive kids in a negative world, parents ask me this question: "Do you go to schools to inspire and motivate kids?" The answer is "Yes". Parents recommend that I should go to every school possible. My response is: "Yes, I do motivate kids, but it is the school that makes the final decision on whether or not I can come and motivate their students."

If you feel that it would be a great idea for me to come and motivate your kids in their school, go ahead and recommend my workshop to the decision maker of that school or private organization. Many times, it is the Community Liaison, Parent Coordinator, the Principal, or event coordinator who makes the decision.

My story of overcoming adversity impacts them. Coming from the sugar cane fields of Guatemala to becoming a published author was not an easy task, especially because of my upbringing.

I also speak in corporations, colleges, private organizations, churches, and every place where there are parents and/or entrepreneurs. Feel free to acquire a book as a gift for your loved one.

What do I talk about when I motivate kids? I tell them my personal story. Once I have connected with them, I tell them what they want to hear and blend with it what they need to hear. Overcoming adversity is a huge element in my talks because when kids are in school, there are so many adversities for them to overcome that if they are not inspired and/or motivated to go through the finish line, they will quit.

You do not want your kid to be a drop out. Neither do I. I want you to be able to be at peace knowing your kid is getting the necessary motivation and information for his or her transformation.

Record your important thoughts and ideas about what you learned overall from this great book. Share it with your friends.
www.Facebook.com/OVinspires

Record your important thoughts and ideas about what you learned overall from this great book. Share it with your friends.

www.Facebook.com/OVinspires

Record your important thoughts and ideas about what you learned overall from this great book.
Share it with your friends.
www.Facebook.com/OVinspires

Record your important thoughts and ideas about you learned overall from this great book. Share it with your friends.
www.Facebook.com/OVinspires

ABOUT THE AUTHORS

Coach "Marilu" Gonzalez has spent the last ten years building a competitive Women's Soccer Program at South Suburban College and Thornwood High School, both in South Holland, IL. Coach Marilu has been part of the soccer community since 1994, playing for Chicago Latin American Soccer Association throughout Chicago and the suburbs, and coaching with the IWSL and NISL, and head coaching at both the local high school district and the local community college. She has coached players from four years old to young adults. Soccer is her passion but coaching is her life.

She is a teacher at Thornton High School, and is a graduate of Chicago State University and Concordia University, where she earned a B.S. in Physical Education and M.A. Educational Leadership, respectively. Coach Marilu has developed high caliber players who have received many awards and have continued their soccer careers at four year universities. The Women's Soccer Program at SSC and TW combines academics and sport to develop students into student athletes. Success is not only evident in athletics but also in academics; our Lady Bulldogs have brought in hundreds of A's! Coach Marilu describes her philosophy as "applying all team skills to real life situations and expecting excellence on and off the field."

Ovidilio D. Vásquez is a leading authority on motivation. He enjoys delivering motivational speeches for parents and youth. He is also the founder of Speak Performance International. Ovidilio came to United States in 2006 from the sugar cane fields of Aldea (village) El Chontel of La Gomera Escuintla Guatemala.

He started to learn English in 2008 at a suburban high school. Even though his mom left him all alone in 2009 due to an emergency, Ovidilio D. Vásquez worked swing shifts in warehouses to support himself through high school and was able to graduate in 2011.

Once he graduated, Ovidilio received Business Management classes from Chabot College. In 2013, he founded Speak Performance International and is now traveling across United States, motivating parents and youth, and teaching parents "How to Raise Positive Kids in a Negative World" and teaching youth "How to Overcome Adversity through an Entrepreneurship Mindset."

Ovidilio is the creator of the revolutionary program "Author in 90 days", a program for professionals who want to tell their story, who want to lead in their field, who believe they have a book in them, who want to leave a legacy for their future generations, and who want their signature to become an autograph. If this is you, Ovidilio is right person to guide you.

Dynamic
Motivational Keynote

$250 OFF

Use this certificate bonus towards your next Motivational Keynote from Ovidilio D. Vasquez

Tel: 510.999.6501

Call NOW

OVinspires.com

Only one bonus certificate may be use at a time.
Other terms and conditions may apply as company policy are subject to change.

Speak Performance Int'l, LLC

Made in the USA
Middletown, DE
22 February 2023

25081543R00068